ROSEN ✔ *Verified*
CURRENT ISSUES

GUN VIOLENCE

Ellen Scherer

ROSEN
PUBLISHING
New York

Published in 2021 by The Rosen Publishing Group, Inc.
29 East 21st Street, New York, NY 10010

Editor: Amanda Vink
Book Design: Reann Nye

Photo Credits: Cover D-Keine/iStock/Getty Images Plus/Getty Images; Series Art PinkPueblo/Shutterstock.com; p. 5 bakdc/Shutterstock.com; p. 7 Cheryl Casey/Shutterstock.com; p. 9 Portland Press Herald/Getty Images; p. 10 Agence France Presse/AFP/Getty Images; p. 11 Keystone/Hulton Archive/Getty Images; p. 12 Jessica McGowan/ Getty Images News/Getty Images; p. 15 Nic Neufeld/Shutterstock.com; p. 17 Hill Street Studios/DigitalVision/Getty Images; p. 19 Joe Sohm/Visions of America/Universal Images Group/Getty Images; p. 21 Kiattipong/Shutterstock.com; p. 23 Ralph Morse/The LIFE Images Collection/ Getty Images; p. 25 Pool/Getty Images News/Getty Images; p. 26 Jeff Swensen/Getty Images News/ Getty Images; p. 29 Salienko Evgenii/Shutterstock.com; p. 31 Sebastiano Tomada/Getty Images News/ Getty Images; p. 32–33 MediaNews Group/Long Beach Press-Telegram via Getty Images/ MediaNews Group/Getty Images; p. 35 Kevin Winter/Getty Images Entertainment/Getty Images; p. 37 Sarah Morris/ Getty Images Entertainment/Getty Images; p. 39 Zach Gibson/Getty Images News/ Getty Images; p. 40 Antonio Guillem/Shutterstock.com; p. 43 Image Source/Getty Images; p. 45 Ethan Miller/Getty Images News/Getty Images.

Library of Congress Cataloging-in-Publication Data

Names: Scherer, Ellen, author.
Title: Gun violence / Ellen Scherer.
Description: New York : Rosen Publishing, [2021] | Series: Rosen verified: current issues | Includes index.
Identifiers: LCCN 2020002895 | ISBN 9781499468403 (paperback) | ISBN 9781499468410 (library binding)
Subjects: LCSH: Gun control–United States–Juvenile literature. | Firearms–Law and legislation–United States–Juvenile literature.
Classification: LCC HV7435 .S34 2021 | DDC 364.150973–dc23
LC record available at https://lccn.loc.gov/2020002895

Manufactured in the United States of America

Some of the images in this book illustrate individuals who are models. The depictions do not imply actual situations or events.

CPSIA Compliance Information: Batch #BSR20. For Further Information contact Rosen Publishing, New York, New York at 1-800-237-9932.

Find us on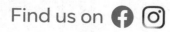

CONTENTS

A HARD PROBLEM TO SOLVE

America knows gun violence is a problem. Many people are killed and injured from gun violence each year. In 2017 alone, 39,773 people died from gun-related injuries in the United States.

Owning guns—and not owning guns—is something many Americans feel very strongly about. Because of that, gun violence is a hard problem to solve. We disagree about what causes it. We deeply disagree about what can fix it. But gun violence affects us all, no matter how different we are. That's why it's important to understand the issue. That way, you can be a part of the answer. You can make your voice heard, and, when you're eighteen and older, vote for leaders who will take action.

More people are affected by gun violence each year.

UNDERSTANDING THE SECOND AMENDMENT

Why do Americans have guns in the first place? The right to own guns is written into American laws. The lawful right to keep guns is stated in the Second Amendment of the Constitution. This is part of the Bill of Rights, which lists the **inherent** rights of every American citizen.

The Founding Fathers wrote this amendment to the Constitution after the American Revolution. They believed citizens should protect themselves in case the government tried to take away their rights.

✓ **VERIFIED**
To find out more about the Constitution, explore this U.S. government official website:
https://www.whitehouse.gov/about-the-white-house/the-constitution/

The Second Amendment is important,
but it's also a little confusing. Let's break it down:

A well-regulated Militia,
- The **militia** should have rules.
- The militia should be organized, or planned.

being necessary to the security of a free State,
- The militia was formed to help keep Americans free.

The right of the people to keep and bear Arms,
- American citizens have the right to own and use guns.

shall not be infringed.
- This right can't be taken away.

You can understand the Second Amendment in two ways. You can argue it protects individual citizens. You can argue it protects the United States.

Some people think the personal right to own a gun is most important. Some people think owning guns is only for when the country is in danger. These different views are one reason Americans disagree about gun ownership.

THE 2ND AMENDMENT PROTECTS INDIVIDUALS

Americans can buy and own guns. They can travel with the guns they buy. They can use them how and when they want.

THE 2ND AMENDMENT PROTECTS THE UNITED STATES

Americans can buy and own guns. It's their duty to protect their country. They have to be ready to fight in a militia.

FAST FACT

GUN CONTROL MEANS A SET OF RULES THAT CONTROL THE MAKING OF, SALE, AND POSSESSION OF FIREARMS.

The Gadsden flag was created by American colonists who wanted independence from Britain during the American Revolution. Today, many people who oppose gun control wave the flag.

A BRIEF HISTORY OF THE NRA

The National Rifle Association (NRA) is an American gun rights group. They lobby for gun ownership. But they didn't always oppose gun control.

The NRA backed gun restrictions, or limits, in the 1960s. This was after John F. Kennedy and Martin Luther King Jr. died from gun violence.

FAST FACT
LOBBYING MEANS TO ATTEMPT TO SWAY POLITICAL OPINION.

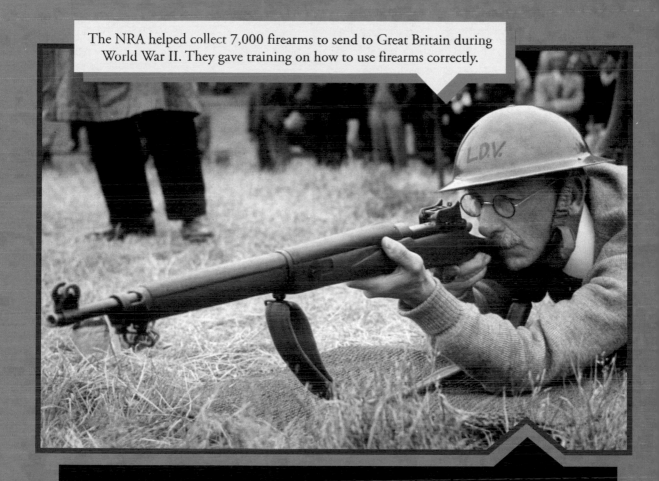

The NRA helped collect 7,000 firearms to send to Great Britain during World War II. They gave training on how to use firearms correctly.

The NRA became more political in the 1970s. The government believed NRA member Kenyon Ballew broke the law by owning unrecorded firearms. The government raided, or suddenly took over, his home. Police officers found illegal weapons. They also shot Ballew in the head. He was **paralyzed** for life.

The NRA started the Institute for Legislative Action (ILA) in 1975. They publicly opposed gun control.

GUN VIOLENCE STUDIES

In 1996, the NRA pushed Congress to stop the Centers for Disease Control (CDC) from studying gun control. This was done with an amendment to a bill. People call it the Dickey Amendment. It's named after its author, Jay Dickey. The amendment said no funds could be used to advance gun control. Once a bill goes through, it becomes law.

President Obama signed an executive order for the CDC to study gun violence in 2013. He asked for $10 million. Research is expensive but helpful. We know a lot more than we did 20 years ago.

✓ VERIFIED

The CDC is a health institute, or a place for study, headquartered in Atlanta, Georgia. It's paid for by the government. Here is the official website:
https://www.cdc.gov.

WHY DO PEOPLE OWN GUNS?

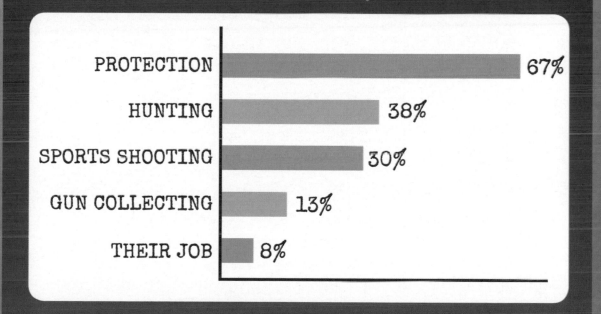

PROTECTION	67%
HUNTING	38%
SPORTS SHOOTING	30%
GUN COLLECTING	13%
THEIR JOB	8%

This graph shows the results of a poll. It shows the reasons why adults in America choose to own a gun. Some people had more than one answer.

GUN VIOLENCE RISK FACTORS

Firearm injuries can happen by accident. In the past twenty years, the number of **unintentional** shootings has dropped by 48 percent. Experts say there are multiple reasons. There's been a drop in the number of people who keep guns at home. More states have laws about gun storage within homes. There is also more gun safety education.

STAY SAFE AROUND GUNS

- Assume, or expect, all guns are loaded.
- Tell someone if you see a gun.
- Don't pick it up.
- Don't point guns at people.

 **VERIFIED**
For information about gun safety, visit:
www.safefirearmsstorage.org

GUN LOCK

IF YOU PRACTICE SHOOTING SPORTS:

1. Don't put your finger on the trigger unless you are about to fire the gun.

2. Protect your ears and eyes.

3. Lock all guns in a safe when not in use.

4. Store all bullets or shells away from guns.

5. Learn federal and state gun laws.

GUN SAFETY FOR YOUNG ADULTS

What has been on the rise in the United States has been intentional gun violence. There have been more than 2,000 mass shootings since 2012. In 2017, there were 39,773 gun-related deaths. Six out of ten were suicides, or when someone takes their own life.

Gun violence is a problem in the United States. But why do people use guns to harm themselves or others?

U.S. GUNS

A 2017 Pew Research Center study found:

- Most gun deaths were in Texas.
- Most gun murders involved handguns.
- 30 percent of American adults said they owned a gun.
- 55 percent of American adults have never owned a gun.
- 59 percent of American adults have friends with guns.
- 72 percent of American adults have fired a gun.

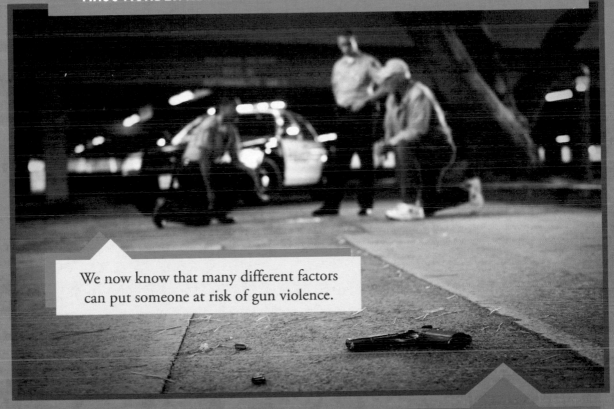

We now know that many different factors can put someone at risk of gun violence.

RISKS FOR GUN VIOLENCE

- Behavior
- Age
- Access to Guns
- Gender Stereotypes
- Race
- Community
- Social Class
- Social Media
- Music
- Video Games

AGGRESSIVE BEHAVIOR

Gun violence is often caused by **aggression**. Some things make aggression more likely. A person may see aggression as normal if they grew up seeing it. Mental illness or the use of drugs and alcohol may also make a person use aggressive behavior.

People sometimes use aggression to show anger and other feelings. This is normal behavior in **adolescence**. But it puts young adults at a greater risk for gun violence. Many people learn problem-solving skills as they get older.

TWO KINDS OF AGGRESSION

IMPULSIVE AGGRESSION

Impulsive aggression is not planned. It usually comes from strong emotions, such as anger. This can happen when two people are fighting.

INSTRUMENTAL AGGRESSION

Instrumental aggression is planned. It's a means to an end—for example, a thief shoots someone in order to get their belongings.

Young people are **disproportionately** affected by gun violence.

PROTECT CHILDREN NOT GUNS!

PERCENTAGE OF DEATHS IN 2016 BY AGE AND CAUSE

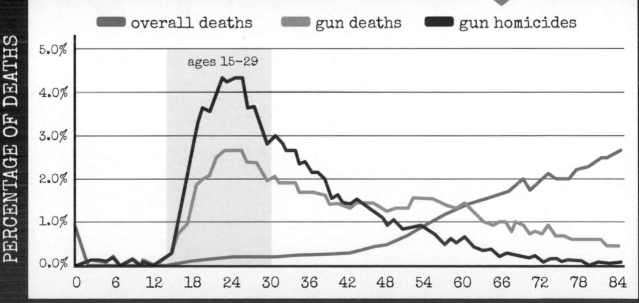

overall deaths · gun deaths · gun homicides

ages 15-29

PERCENTAGE OF DEATHS

5.0%
4.0%
3.0%
2.0%
1.0%
0.0%

0 6 12 18 24 30 36 42 48 54 60 66 72 78 84

AGE

ACCESS TO GUNS

Some families have guns in their homes. This is allowed by the Second Amendment. But some families don't store their guns safely. They may not use safety devices or locked storage holders.

Laws about gun storage differ from state to state. There are no federal standards for locking devices. But in October 2005, Congress passed a law. It became unlawful for guns dealers to sell a handgun without a safety or storage device.

FAST FACT
THE NATIONAL INSTITUTE OF JUSTICE (NIJ) FINANCED STUDIES FOR THE SMART GUN. THE SMART GUN IS MADE TO FIT AND WORK FOR ONLY ONE PERSON. RIGHT NOW THIS GUN ISN'T DEPENDABLE. YET IF IT CAN BE MADE TO WORK, THE SMART GUN COULD REDUCE THE RISK OF GUN VIOLENCE FOR MANY PEOPLE.

Studies have shown that just seeing a gun can make a person more violent. It can cause people to act on problems with aggression. This is called the weapons effect.

GENDER STEREOTYPES

Many cultures value aggressive behavior in boys. This is a gender stereotype. This is when a society expects someone to look or act in a certain way based on their gender. Aggressive behavior can lead to gun violence.

FALSE BELIEF #1

Boys and men aren't supposed to show emotion.

Emotions are natural. They are a very important part of the human experience. They allow us to understand ourselves and others. They help us to make decisions. There is no wrong way to feel.

FALSE BELIEF #2

Boys and men should be tough. They don't have to ask for help.

People who don't ask for help when they need it are more likely to try to take control in other ways. They may do this using aggressive behavior. This is especially true when they feel threatened.

Toy guns were once far more popular than they are today. "Cops and robbers" was a common game for boys to play.

STAYING SAFE?

Many people own guns because they want to be safe. However, the FBI says violent crime and property crime rates have been falling for two decades.

Many people carry guns with them to feel safer too. In 2016, nearly 13 million Americans got permits to carry concealed handguns. Boys and men in Chicago were asked about guns in 2017. They believed everyone around them was carrying guns. They thought they should also carry guns.

Becoming A Man—Sports Edition is a counseling and **mentoring** program. It taught students in Chicago to solve problems without violence. The students were 44 percent less likely to be arrested for a violent crime. Programs like these show violence and carrying guns isn't necessarily the way to keep people safer.

RACE AND CLASS

Populations with higher levels of **poverty** have higher levels of crime. **Minority** communities are more likely to live in poverty. They often face job **discrimination**. This keeps families in poverty.

Minority communities are more at risk for gun violence too. They are also more likely to be victims of gun violence. Just one example of this happened in 2018. A **synagogue** in Pittsburgh was attacked during morning services.

POVERTY BY ETHNICITY

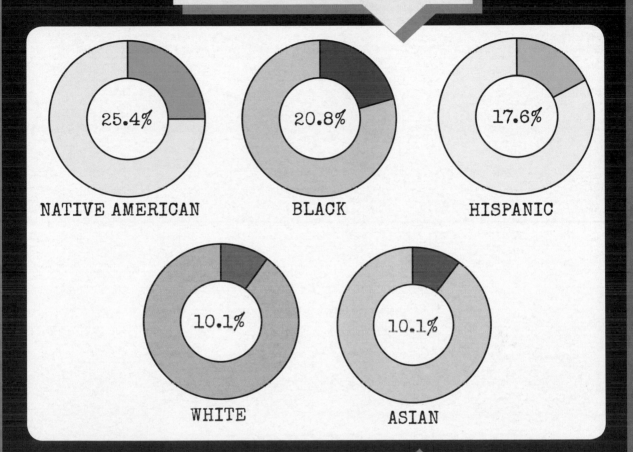

NATIVE AMERICAN
25.4%

BLACK
20.8%

HISPANIC
17.6%

WHITE
10.1%

ASIAN
10.1%

In 2018, the highest poverty rates by race were experienced by Native American and black populations in the United States. That means that a disproportionate amount of these people were living in poverty.

PUBLIC POLICY

Black Americans are more likely to be arrested and tried in court for a violent crime. Some government **policies** have led to this problem. Rudy Giuliani was elected mayor of New York City in 1993. He promised to clean up the streets with the "broken windows" idea.

This idea led to stop and frisk. This allows police officers to stop, question, and search citizens. Citizens only need to look "suspicious." Michael Bloomberg backed this policy after he was elected New York City mayor in 2001. He said the policy would reduce the number of guns on the street.

PROBLEMS

There are problems with stop and frisk.
No guidelines led to:

- Racial profiling
- Overpolicing
- Distrust of police
- Police misconduct

In 2013, the New York Civil Liberties Union reported police found 397 guns during 191,851 stop and frisk encounters. That's 0.2 percent.

WHAT'S THE BROKEN WINDOWS THEORY?

A theory, or idea, often called the broken windows theory says that when a community has many things that are broken or out of order (such as windows), it's a sign people don't care about the community. That means more crime may take place there. After this idea spread, police started arresting more people for smaller things, such as graffiti. There was also a drop in more serious crimes. Now, however, some people think this was caused by other factors.

POLICE GUN VIOLENCE

There is distrust of police by minority groups. Why this distrust? Officers have a history of using excessive force. This means a police officer uses a stronger amount of force than usual. They do it to protect themselves or others from harm. It has ended in many needless gun deaths, though.

BLACK LIVES MATTER

Black Lives Matter is an organization that works to end violence and **racism** against African American communities. Activists with the Black Lives Matter movement have called for justice against police brutality, or the use of excessive force. For example, many demanded that police wear body cameras to record all interactions.

POLICE-RELATED GUN VIOLENCE

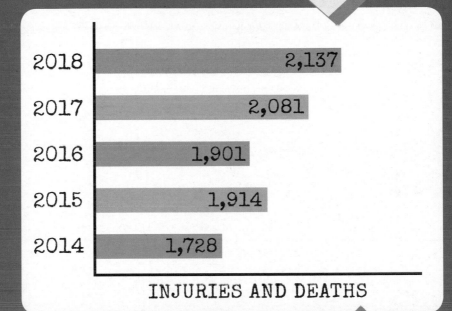

Year	Injuries and Deaths
2018	2,137
2017	2,081
2016	1,901
2015	1,914
2014	1,728

INJURIES AND DEATHS

The numbers in this graph show injuries and deaths of police suspects from 2014 to 2018.

In 2014, 18-year-old unarmed Michael Brown was shot at least six times by a police officer in Ferguson, Missouri. His body was left for hours on the street. This event sparked national protests.

Police are at risk for gun violence. They carry a gun all the time. Their job is unsafe. They work long hours and witness upsetting crimes. Some of them end up with mental health issues. This puts them at risk for suicide with a gun.

A least five New York Police Department officers commit suicide each year. Los Angeles, Chicago, and Houston have lowered police suicide numbers with better mental health services.

FAST FACT

IN ADDITION TO PHYSICAL DRILLS, AS DEPICTED HERE, MANY POLICE FORCES NOW REQUIRE OFFICERS TO ENGAGE IN SENSITIVITY TRAINING. THIS TRAINING HELPS OFFICERS HANDLE HIGH-RISK SITUATIONS.

VIDEO GAMES AND MUSIC

Two teenagers killed 13 people and injured 20 at Columbine High School in 1999. Then they took their own lives. People knew they played violent video games. Many Americans linked violent video games with gun violence.

It's unclear if violent video games relate to gun violence. Some people think first-person shooter games blur reality and fiction. Others think aggressive people are more drawn to these games in the first place. Some think there is too much focus on video games. They want other actions.

Childish Gambino uses his music to comment on gun violence, like the Charleston church shooting in 2016.

MUSIC AND VIOLENCE

Many Americans also see a connection between gun violence and hip-hop and rap music. It has a complicated history. Many musicians promote violence, alcohol, and drugs in their music. For some listeners, this can make violence normal. Other artists **criticize** the use of violence in society.

SOCIAL MEDIA AND MASS SHOOTINGS

Mass shootings are not the most common cases of gun violence. But they are highly covered by the media. One reason for this is an increase in social media use. There was no social media in 1999. That means a lot of people didn't know about the shooting at Columbine until the day after it happened.

The shooting in Parkland, Florida, at Marjory Stoneman Douglas High School in 2018 was much different. Students used social media to record video during the shooting. They used it to contact friends and family. The public knew about the shooting right away.

FAST FACT

DRILLS AND LOCKDOWNS ARE COMMON IN SCHOOLS TODAY. SOME PEOPLE WORRY THAT THESE PRACTICE DRILLS ARE **TRAUMATIC** FOR STUDENTS.

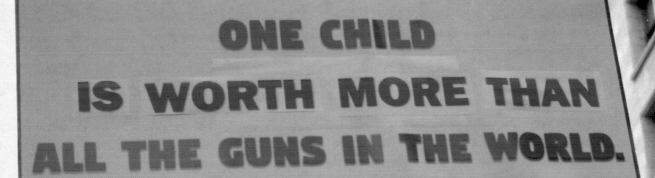

Parkland students used social media to plan the March for Our Lives in March 2018. This event took place in Washington, D.C. It started a global talk about gun violence. The students continue to use social media to take an active role in gun violence prevention.

MASS SHOOTINGS AND GUN CONTROL

A school shooting in 2012 also made headlines. Adam Lanza walked into Sandy Hook Elementary School. He shot and killed 20 children, 6 adults, and himself. The children were in first grade.

The parents of these children and one survivor decided to do something. They sued Remington Arms. Remington Arms made the gun Lanza used in the 2012 shooting. In 2019, the Supreme Court did not hear an appeal on the lawsuit. This allowed the case to go to court in 2020.

Many people are tired of hearing politicians respond to gun violence by offering thoughts and prayers. They want policies put in place.

MENTAL ILLNESS AND GUN SUICIDE

More than half of mass shooters struggle with serious mental illness before turning to gun violence. The media tends to focus on this connection. They wondered if Adam Lanza had mental illness. They thought it would explain him going through with the Sandy Hook shooting. The same was thought of James Holmes. He shot and killed 12 people and injured 58 people in a Colorado movie theater.

FAST FACT
AMERICAN CITIZENS WERE ONLY 4.3% OF THE GLOBAL POPULATION IN 2016. YET AMERICANS MADE UP 35.3% OF THE WORLD'S GUN SUICIDES.

Gun violence is still related to mental illness. Suicide is the leading cause of gun violence in the United States. Ninety percent of people who die by suicide struggle with **depression** or another mental illness.

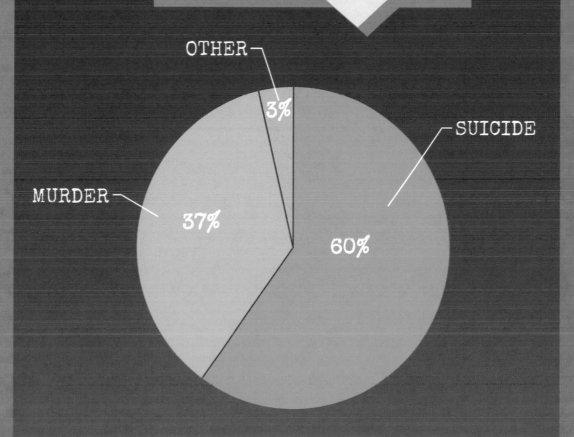

GUN VIOLENCE IN 2016

OTHER — 3%

MURDER — 37%

SUICIDE — 60%

Many people believe mental illness causes mass shootings. There's a problem with this belief. It's too simple. Studies have shown that most people with a serious mental illness are not violent toward others.

GUN SUICIDE PREVENTION

Men have more thoughts of suicide than women. Gender stereotypes may be the cause. Gun suicides are more likely during young adulthood. This is when young men usually start thinking about what it means to be a man. Gun suicides also increase for white men when they retire. They may struggle with having a purpose.

PREVENTING GUN SUICIDE

- no guns in the home
- mental health services
- reduced gun access
- gun permits (licenses)
- waiting periods between buying and getting weapon
- safe storage
- background checks

Gun suicide rates have risen over the last decade, especially for children and teens.

WHAT YOU CAN DO

Gun violence can be prevented. New facts are discovered every day. You can always learn more about risk factors, gun laws, and gun safety. You can use your knowledge to become part of the answer.

HISTORIC GUN DEBATES

1791: Second Amendment is ratified, or made official.

1871: National Rifle Association forms.

1934: National Firearms Act passes.

1938: Federal Firearms Act passes.

1968: Gun Control Act passes.

1975: Institute for Legislative Action (ILA) forms.

1976: Political Victory Fund forms.

1986: Firearm Owners' Protection Act passes.

1994: Violent Crime Control and Law Enforcement Act passes.

2005: Protection of Lawful Commerce in Arms Act passes.

2008: *District of Columbia v. Heller* is argued in the Supreme Court.

2020: *Soto v. Bushmaster* is tried in the Connecticut Supreme Court.

The gun debate has lasted almost 230 years. Hopefully soon, we will figure out how to prevent gun violence in the future.

GLOSSARY

adolescence: The period of time when a child grows into an adult.

aggression: Angry or violent behavior or feelings.

criticize: To find fault with.

depression: A mood disorder marked by sadness and inactivity.

discrimination: The practice of unfairly treating a person or group of people differently from other people.

disproportionate: Being a difference that is not fair, reasonable, or justified.

inherent: Belonging to the basic nature of someone or something.

mentor: To serve as a trusted counselor or guide.

militia: A body of citizens organized for military service.

minority: A part of a population differing from others in some characteristics.

paralyze: To make (a person or animal) unable to move or feel all or part of the body.

policy: A set of guidelines or rules that determine a course of action.

poverty: The state of being poor.

racism: The belief that certain races of people are by birth and nature better than others.

synagogue: The house of worship of a Jewish congregation.

traumatic: To cause someone to become very upset in a way that can lead to serious mental and emotional problems.

unintentional: Not done on purpose.

INDEX